Juices of the Forbidden Fruit
Poetry

Tapuwa Tremor Mapaike

Mwanaka Media and Publishing Pvt Ltd,
Chitungwiza Zimbabwe
*
Creativity, Wisdom and Beauty

Publisher: *Mmap*
Mwanaka Media and Publishing Pvt Ltd
24 Svosve Road, Zengeza 1
Chitungwiza Zimbabwe
mwanaka@yahoo.com
mwanaka13@gmail.com
www.africanbookscollective.com/publishers/mwanaka-media-and-publishing
https://facebook.com/MwanakaMediaAndPublishing/

Distributed in and outside N. America by African Books Collective
orders@africanbookscollective.com
www.africanbookscollective.com

ISBN: 978-1-77928-208-8
EAN: 9781779282088

© Tapuwa Tremor Mapaike 2025

All rights reserved.
No part of this book may be reproduced or transmitted in any form or by any means, mechanical or electronic, including photocopying and recording, or be stored in any information storage or retrieval system, without written permission from the publisher

DISCLAIMER
All views expressed in this publication are those of the author and do not necessarily reflect the views of *Mmap*.

Table of Contents

Grain Of Humanity
The Answer
Prayer beads
We had it all
I Am Not A Line Of Coke
You
Anhedonia
Dear Miracle
Countless Muses
Afterplay
Just A Few Questions
Creature Of Lust
Dim Nightclubs
Breath Of Life
Balls, Son. Balls
Long as
The Fire
"Chipuka"
Noticed
Seriously?
The Thing Is
Don't forget That...
If You Can...
Must We Always Kill?
Avalanches
Bloody Cross Section
Somewhere Between Doomed And Privileged
Vixen
Memory
Appetizing AF
Unhooked

02:57 a.m. Already
Status quo
Preprogrammed
For Hours
If You Cannot Do It For Yourself
Decryption
Becoming "Him"
Wait
Dilemma
December 03
NPCs
Concisely
Got Game?
Consider Yourself Warned
Remember
It's Time
The Ark
Things That Mobilize My Pen
Mmap New African Poets Series

The Preface

Some of these poems were conceived in places that have never known sunlight within me, whilst some of which gained existence on a very public guillotine where viscerally died innocence, fear, anxiety and colonial dogmas. The collection itself is way more than just a book; it's a sweaty whore in your honorable prophet's bed, a surveillance drone sent to hover over your conscience, a cathartic surreptitiously slipped into your soul and a portal into the mind of a perennially licentious thinker. The heavyweight verses and surgical punchlines come with a guarantee to perpetually alter your worldview.

Grain Of Humanity

you won't be the first person to be murdered by nothing
you won't be the first person to be disgusted by what you
do for a living
you won't be the first person to get
seduced by the aura of a forbidden book
you won't be the first person to crave the
distinctive scent which accompanies the
first rain after a dry spell
you won't be the first person to resort to
advanced interrogation techniques
you won't be the first person to
drown in the eyes of a prostitute
you won't be the first person to wake up to some head in
a wrong bed
you won't be the first person to vote in absentia
you won't be the first person to premeditatedly relapse
you won't be the first person to envy the dead
you won't be the first person to ignore the whispers of
the Holy Spirit
you won't be the first person to give false witness under oath
you won't be the first person to raise a stranger's offspring with
a love so strong that God's Kingdom feels eternally indebted to you
you won't be the first person to contemplate suicide on a daily basis

yesterday I woke up around 03.00am and
gracefully sought Allah
His smile betrayed His location

you won't be
the first person to refuse to return someone's soulmate
you won't be

the first person to accidentally sire a
life-changing $3x position
you won't be the first person to regret nutting outside her
you won't be the first person to be posterized in front of your crush
you won't be the first person to be constantly besieged by
the in-laws
you won't be the first person to nearly get away with
orgasmically exorcising the underaged
you won't be the first person to start groping for Christ on a deathbed
you won't be the first person to take cover in music
you won't be the first person to
come back home from a war carrying it in your eyes
you won't be the first person to never attend a
church service unarmoured (not every soul
can flourish in conflagrations)

you won't be the first person to walk away from a beloved drug
you won't be the first person to lust after Arabic territory
you won't be the first person to get knocked up because of
"free beer"
(I'm now approx 3 poontangs away from sunyata) you
won't be the first person to have a
baby mama who thrives on spooking your prey
you won't be the first person to prostrate and pray in a
den of "terrorists"
you won't be the first person to
throw up at an amputation/execution
you won't be the first person to
use an opponent's blood as a prayer mat
you won't be the first person to feel like
you crucified yourself on the wrong sister

you won't be
the first person
to end up fighting to the death against
someone with whom you
should be unsparingly making love...

because timepieces
are better commanders than you and I.
because the ocean (somehow)
has a desirable conscience.
because the carravajios
and the mozarts
of this world
can orgasm perfectly in solitude.
because the prostitute
also bears God's signature.
because you
cannot wait for
an insouciant creature to become respectable.
because we're (all of us) citizens of
gangrenous laughter.
because her body is capable of
triggering mass madness.
because the exporters
of genocide
do not just play chess.
because
not every leaf has a song.
because sometimes there is no shame in
allowing your bodily fluids to BASE jump from
the balconies of your eyes.
because some chests
has never known compersion.

because you
won't be the first person to suffer from psithurismsickness.
because we
have checkmated most of our gods and
the world has never looked more constipated.

The Answer

This is Frazier's thunderous left hook horizontalizing your Ali in the 15th
This is the genesis of a seismic epiphany
This is a stream of consciousness
This is a deep tissue massage
This is a holy regime
This is pollen
This is shrapnel
This is a herd of hippos in your green field
This is the infallible mandingo in your daughter's bedroom

This
is raw action

This is the uterus within which gestate virile political parties and religions
This is the thought of ruling rome in a heart that pumps plebeian blood
This is a constellation in a ballsack (part of it might
end up on your fiancée's cleavage and
eyelashes)
This is guerrilla warfare
This is a stash house
This is a gangbang before monogamy

This is my lovechild with the goddess of...
This is a soul-ensnaring painting stationed on an innocent-looking wall
This is a scroll drenched with juices of the forbidden fruit
This is a pregnant body in need of a midwife and
a lionhearted exorcist

This is the tarpeian rock in the form of mikayla's tongue
This is adultery on a bed of leaves
This is the sculpture after my own heart
This is an endless phalanx of demons+angels
This is your wife's legs wrapped around my waist

This is a viscerally disturbing prophecy
This is a time bomb
What do you know about mauerbauertraurigkeit?
Can you discern spirits?
Can you capitalise on demon possession?
This is persecuted craftsmanship

Because of this
somebody might receive a colombian manicure
or worse

This is costly salvation
This is the goddamned master key
This is not your typical sacrificial lamb
This
is the blood of a divinely knocked up virgin in the 21st century

This is ancient witchcraft fused with
futuristic technology
This is an armoury for eccentrics and the purposefully invisible
This is Helen reincarnated

This (this is a teleportation device)
You're not holding a book
This is an opium den
This is an aphrodisiac (This
is a bonus directly from the gods)

she said "NOW ISN'T THE TIME
FOR YOU TO START CALLING HIM (MY) MAN
HE ALREADY KNOWS YOUR VAGINA AS MUCH AS HE
KNOWS MINE
HE
IS
(OUR)
MAN.
ISN'T THAT HOW YOU VIEW HIM EVERY TIME YOU
GET BUSY ENTERTAINING HIS
STRAY DICK?"

"WHO? ME??? I don't want your m..." the homebreaker
ate an exorcistic jab before finishing her statement.

some spectators pulled out their cameraphones
I got inspired (in my head as well as
in my boxers)

Bitch come and rub that nomadic rump on my lap
This is an underworld refugee camp
This is a "man of God" possessedly swiping things off the table to nail somebody's wife upon it
This is an obese high ranking rat chilling in lotus position on top of a stack of missing drought relief sacks of grain
This is a poker table (welcome to the jungle)
Secrets of the undying One lairs here
This is a plague straight outta the Almighty's lab
This is
no man's land

This

is the life-changing presence of
an illuminated soul, royal blood and
the third member of the notorious trinity (deep
inside you, uninsulated)

Hahaha
This is Eve's weakness
This is
a debonair mamba
orally minister to it before I
methodically cause you the sweetest pain
_Have you ever been plougheD by
an articulate thruster?

Prayer beads

make babies with prostitutes
descend into man-eating gold mines
vote for pyromaniacs
psychoanalyze the demons of your motherland
administer civic education to the ideologically malnutritioned
sink the evangelist's battleships
help your balls to feel like a reposing volcano
plant a tree with a prayer
unprotectedly enter silence

think about
the she-devils you
have survived and give
your ancestors a worthier drink

leave vestiges on multiple continents
learn mind control from God Himself
smoke only the persecuted stuff
outgamble the old testament prophets
(where there is gold to be found
there is no need for you to be frugal with your bodily fluids)
develop a habit of fishing alone
(sometimes the predatory mind isn't interested in
any other prey but its own self) you may use sleep as
a confession booth (I'm thinking
of taking my conductive soul to the wilderness;
I have galaxies to absorb.)
try to marry a praise and worshiper who is
even more dangerous on her knees
never finger anyone you don't intend to tongue
always stay ready to deal with the

side effects of being a ruminant soul

your psyche is no mystery
it has long been articulately spread on a page somewhere
disvirgin as many poems and novels as you can

skepticism might just prolong your days (acting is an
extremely important lifeskill)
invariably treat great questions the same way you would
bioweapons
refuse to be satisfied by cleaner answers
skillfully assess widows' legs at the funerals of
their husbands
(the pangs of artbirth will alchemize your core)
meditate in the rain
meticulously milk circumcised theologians
fall in love with her thorns (it's a risk worthy taking)
lick (and sssuck) her trigger until she recoils
if she's endowed with
a cleavage that can swallow up a pendant;
TAKE ADVANTAGE (yes dummy, get a -job)
find someone with an inked spine and
pollockianly land your lava flows on it (I know you're a doggy
person)
just make sure that cupid doesn't leave you with a fatal wound
you may confide in pregnant clouds (the post of
a "man" showing off his painted nails
just gained a million more reactions than that of
GENOCIDE in PALESTINE.
Nxa! today was a very disgusting day)

Hey! use these prayer beads correctly.

We had it all

desires to give up
traffic lights to ignore
influencers to mistrust
regimes to deracinate
civilizations to exhume/decode
luminaries to fast and pray for
fuck buddies and religions to juggle
puke to revisit
footage to expunge
rumours to starve to death
hours of equanimity to freedive into
judges to threaten
mountains to conquer
free high definition adult entertainment to consume
prescriptions to abuse
weight to push
celebrities to eyefuck
songs to fall in love with over and over again

the need for human shields with
sizzling time machines at
the convergence of their thighs

exotic dancers to use as cocaine
war criminals to sacrifice
corporates to dismantle
imperialists to outthink and outwork
affluent perverts to turn down respectfully
poems to tranfuse into our bloodstreams
prisons to visit bearing gifts

constitutions to open-mindedly revise
shrines to rebuild
squirting medicine to wholesale
contraceptive methods to abolish
preconceptions to purge
bananas to duct tape to a wall when million$ needed shampooing
intel to torture out of people
courtesans to ravish (hours before the night climaxed
her coochie was already smelling like a postrace racetrack)

skin lightening products to resort to in order to make it in a
society that obstinately refused to tolerate strong melanin
(especially
in straight people)

manifestos to burn
elephants to dildo using needles and toothpicks
exposés to share
eye-opening trees to make love to
slay queens to pass around like calabashes of mqombothi
space to explore / planets to colonize
oceans to reparate
governments to install
archbishops to investigate
policies to terminate

we had it all (and some among us even got away with
barebacking the unborn)
we were pilgrims vacillating between fuckfests
we were the disfigured bodies in bombed cities
we were the happily cuckolded
we were the reliable firing squad
we were the vulture's brothers and sisters

there were times when
it felt so damn good to be particles of
dust in a demonic whirlwind
and times when democratic mentality
could earn you a death uglier than Christ's

treasuries to syphon
erotica to zoom
doctrines to regurgitate
inner engineering to make time for
the pomodoro technique to employ
(she was precious because she
was a sprinkler with ridiculous commentatory skills
she was precious because of the way she
could take it in all three portals
she was precious because
gambling was her religion)

balls
to refill
NPCs to exploit
childhood wings to miss
senate hearings to prepare for
baby mamas and hangovers to survive
perfumed hairs of the night to lose our sanity to
security agencies that eat their own to avoid
thermal images to snipe
openly immoral martyrs to counter
mouths to sadomasochistically ransack
a list of felonies to wed before the dusk of every epoch
commercial spacewalks to complete
killing licenses to consummate

till operaters to flirt with
gamblers to tax
tithing receipts to bulwark our properties with
mountains to hurl to the foreigners' hammermills
comrades and soulmates to extricate from the world wide WEB
lovers to leisurely
create electrical currents with (my vestige on her ticklish neck,
my fingerprints on her amenable spine, my residue in her tasty depths...
I don't think I would have done half the
things I did to her if she
was exclusively mine
my possessors went apeshit whenever she
dared enter their domain wearing that consecrated ring
her sinfulness uniquely charged my core.) we
were privileged junkies.

I Am Not A Line Of Coke

I am not an uncircumcised "pagan"
I am not capable of disgracing my katana
I am not a faithless gambler

all ye amphibious daughters of men_
come
and ride me all night
come
and ride me till your ancestors wail
come
and ride me until regimes devour their founders

I am neither rain nor the
temptatious scent that comes along with it

I am not one of the builders of Rome
I am not an idolater
I am not a blood drinker
I am not a slave master
I am not a rainbow person
I am not God's mistake

I've
never been to the summit of mount everest, but
I have been a serious stoner (experiencing rebirth with every pull)

I am not an arms merchant
the only friend in high places that I can count on is
an iconoclastic alien who took off from earth (with
decorated palms) more than two thousand years ago

I am not one of kiki's victims
I am not a big game hunter
I am not a coup d'etat plotter
I am not a marijuana farmer (but
it's something I once tried) I am
not a strip club owner
I am not a member of
any secret society (which might
change soon)

I am not the commander of any army
I am not an apple tree
my poetry doesn't rouse everybody
and I don't feel guilty for breaking most of
these muse's hearts because I
never ask them to open their chests for me (unless
of course her twins has what it takes to
cast a spell on my subconscious)

I am not the creator of jet kun do, but
if you feel like you can knock me out
know that I always accept challenges

I am not a contract killer
I am not an anarchist (my
understanding of humanity forbids)
I am not your confidant
I do not even have the concoction you need to
terminate that pregnancy
_nonetheless, think twice princess

I am not nonhalal (but,
please, NO teeth)

I am not a line of coke
I am not the antidote for any poison
I am not a snake charmer (I'm very much
allergic to snitches)

I
am
not an angel of anything
not your shrinker
not your masseur
not your horse

but I sure can SERVICE you senselessly

hydrate that body before requesting me
I am not a medic
and I am NOT necrophiliac

(hey Mrs...?? may you please shroud your cornigerous duo
my mind can still use a team of fully equipped janitors and
I will never be joseph.)

I am not your ideal martyr
I am not north's father

of course I am a french kisser
I only haven't kissed anissa kate
and I ain't villon

I am not an oasis
I possess inexhaustible infernos and edens within me

I am not an abomination
I'm just a tapestry of necessary heresies

I am not the flag-bearer you're looking for
this time around if I end up back inside her, I
might not be able to forgive myself ever again

I have relapsed way more than I've acknowledged my addictions
I am not prey in search of a predator

cougars over nymphets
I am not Vladimir Nabokov
does mermaids also have what our females possess...
if they do
I'd like to... Uh...

I am not a voyeur
with a pair of binoculars and an eidetic memory

some ideas approach me with an armed marching band
and some pokes me with their sportive high voltage nipples.
last month there was an idea which decided to
use bedroom eyes on me (I ended up writing a
short novel about an asshole that metamorphed into a famous pussy.)

I am not an aquarium of obsessions
I am not an incubator of grudges
I am not your first lady's heaviest secret
the watch on my wrist can't step in the ring with your lifetime income
I am not a jealousy sex demon
make eye contact with me and repent

I am not xuanzang's pilgrimage
I have a lot in common with Noah's flood

I am not ouchea tryna fall in love
you're in the presence of a prescient bait-taker

I'm the type that refuses to pedestal people just because they're dead
I'm the type that cannot pay a whore depending on her butt size
I'm the type that pray for one's own enemies with both eyes open
I'm the type that feast on pussy dialoguing with it
I'm the type that enjoys psychoanalyzing the ones all others go to for guidance

I'm the type that prefers turnin' Up alone, my
head is a teeming planet
I'm the type that carries rubbers to a church conference
my heart is cold but saved (take a look at how animals
are drawn to me)
I'm the type that studies in night clubs and ruminate on park benches
I'm the type that uses libraries as time machines
I'm a troubled beast with a collection of socially acceptable masks
I know what I want and I
never expect the universe to go down on me
I'm the type that favors a companion who
understands how satanic parasitism is

I have serious animalistic instincts
I'm the type that doesn't mind judging a book by its cover (and/or scent)
I'm the type that can scrupelessly use a sin as a stepping stone

I am not a nobel price winner
I am not a drug dealer
I am not a presidential candidate
but
DON'T EVER
make the mistake of thinking you can get away with
the felony of jizzing on my brand.

You

ever creampied another man's wife?
ever been shocked by the eyes in the mirror?
ever contemplated seppuku?
ever preprogrammed your brain before going to bed?
ever been on a cunthunt?
ever wet the pages of a work of fiction?
ever tongue kissed death?
ever woke up to an avalanche of strong messages?
ever been terrified of going back home to your family?
ever been the guy they only remember when their
sewers are misbehaving?
ever been sucked by an alphette?
ever ruptured someone's womb on purpose?
ever had the fortune of living like a dead man?
ever witnessed something that took away your
ability to aidlessly fall asleep?

ever been preceded by a butt plug?
ever been bukkake'd by your past?
ever overshared in your sleep?
ever woke up metamorphed?
ever defended a demon?
ever been a rimmer?

do not love the limelight so damn much;
fame is an inveterate @$$f?ck+r
do not love orgasms so damn much;
you might attract legions of the defenestrated
do not love the dance floor so damn much;
you might lose a spouse
do not love the clouds so damn much;

you might od
do not love the doctors so damn much;
you might unnecessarily get robbed of
your peace of mind
do not love thy neighbor so damn much;
your dirty laundry might easily make it to the marketplace
do not love the truth so damn much;
you might blaspheme

everybody has insecurities (otherwise
lucipher would still be in his Father's Kingdom.)

you do know that Tyson could have easily
annihilated Paul, right?
you do know that we must
finish what Gaddafi started, right?
you do know that LBJ
has long earned the right to sit on that iron throne, right?
you do know that tebogo's victory at the 2024 olympic games
made lyles feel PUBLICLY cuckolded, right?
you do know that your wife is pledgeable, too,
right?
you do know that your savior also has guilty pleasures, right?

you do know that not every blunt dreams of being a cigar, right?
you do know that walking barefooted is not the
only way to exchange electrons with the surface of our planet,
right?
you do know that the finest mental patients speaks in parables,
right?

you do know
that some referees are useless, right?

you do know that your vote is alterable, right?
you do know that this is a glory hole, right?
you do know that you're being f?ck!d, right?
you do know (don't you?)
that one punchline
is all it takes
for you to be irreversibly infected

ever regretted an act of faith?
ever felt like a ticking bomb?
ever gave your Creator an ultimatum?
ever been skewered (ass to mouth) by your clan?
ever paid someone to confirm your freaking suspicions?
ever been penalized for something you had already atoned for?

ever been relegated to the couch?
ever had to turn down an extremely seductive award?
ever spent an entire year on the road to
bury one loved one after another?
ever offered blood money in church?
ever dungeoned yourself to protect the world?

when you work
_work like extraterrestrials.
when you fuck
_Fuck like panthers.
when you cuddle
_cuddle like reptiles.
when you fight
_fight like chimpanzees.
when you have mastered something
_innovately simplify it.

when you dance
_do it like conquerers of melancholy.
when you mourn
_mourn like pilgrims out of the freaking void.
when you avenge
_become record breaking plagues
and when you choose silence
_

Anhedonia

when I'm cracking a jewel out of its cradle
when I'm
pushing a new project's panties to the side
when I'm defenseless deep inside somebody I adore
when I'm drawing something I won't either sell or hang
when I'm swapping views with
an addictive muse
when I'm onstage
when I'm in the booth
when I'm in the gluteal cleft of unaffable mountains
when I'm landscaping at my parents' place
when I'm in the trenches for a cause I
can unhesitatingly sacrifice majority of you for

when I'm cooperating in
the Lord's house

when I'm mindfully stargazing
when I'm perambulating the labia of a lake during fishing season
when I'm foreplaying with my death-spitting workmate
when I'm placing something valuable
in the hands of a challenged soul begging on the pavement
when I'm concentrating on
a very enthralling seminude dancer doing her thang to my
favorite jam of all time
when I'm lacing my most expensive kicks
when I'm braaing for my better half
when I'm playing with my nieces
when I'm practicing a combat sport
when I'm building a fierce poem in solitude

when I'm practicing archeology on a widow
when I'm craving nonhalal
when I'm doing skin to skin with
a sweaty milf with sapiosexual demons
when I'm designing breathtaking architectural stuff
when I'm posted on a balcony (playing the
philosophical observer)

when I'm stalking someone I'm not yet ready to let go

when I'm rolling a joint
when I'm disciplining my demons
when I'm making eye contact with my prey
when I'm feeding a voyeuress' soul
when she start making supplication unto my veined cannon
when I'm discovering that she's almost still virgo intacta
when I'm deconsecrating another man's wife
when I'm making the ATM cuuuuuum

I no longer feel the same fire that I used to feel in these bones.

Dear Miracle

will wearing original jewellery make me happy?
will many children with a God-fearing wife
make me happy?
will book sales overseas and
prolific livestock make me happy?
will turning my art into currency at the speed of light supercharge me
will fine dining and latest gadgets make me happy?
will gambling with my bosses' boss make me happy?
will life in the diaspora
make me
happy?
will early retirement make me happy?
will ditching this barret improve my lustre?

will three hundred and sixty-six concubines and a
mine touched by ma'fuckin midas make me happy?
will sharing a doobie with the Queen of... make me happy?
will castrating my enemies make me happy?
will axing your ribs and feeding your lungs to the vultures
make me happy?
will taking somebody's wife's @nal v!rginity make me happy?
will irrigating my fields with your blood give me peace of mind?

will exposing the witch within the family make me happy?
will watching my fiancée performing on top of another man fill my
bones with the sweetest electricity?
will forsaking all others for a sapphist improve my mental health?
will bonding with the mountains and
sleeping directly under all those
twinkling exit wounds restore me?

will detonating in your beloved cousin's mouth make me happy?
will idly waiting for the world to burn and drown make me happy?
will attending the remaining years of this masquerade with my
real face make me happy?
will louis vuitton bedsheets and
internationally recognized underwear make me happy?
will bulking up make me happy?
will using an electric toothbrush make me happy?
will traveling with a bloody convoy make me happy?
will installing CCTVs around all my properties lessen my paranoia?
will having high ranking members of the police in my
pocket make me happy?
will insuring my cock make me happy?
will knocking a student pastor up put a permanent smile on my
face?
will wearing a four hundred dollar cologne make me happy?
will sleeping with a glock under my pillow make me happy?

maybe I should just do whatever the oracle says I must in order to
timely touch my first milli
dammit! maybe I should just sacrifice you and yours
maybe I should just upgrade my venom
maybe I should just resort to bellicism
wait, maybe I should just
let my enemies do the dirty work for me
maybe I should just get in bed with all the apex predators

maybe I should just find a good seat from which to
watch them eat each other alive
maybe I should just feed their brains to my dogs,
use their spouses to appreciate my vassals
and their daughters to revitalize my blood

maybe I should just unleash the iconoclast in me
maybe I should just get 66,6% of my body inked
maybe I should just start gambling way smarter than
that biblical dude (hagar's baby daddy)

sketching and shadow boxing truly helps me conduct these
voices in my head
maybe I should stop dodging the asylum

maybe I should start spending more time working on
my prose while absorbing all kinds of soothing music
maybe I should try to relax in a swimming pool under this October sun
maybe I should soak myself in prayer
maybe I should start subsisting on live prey
maybe I should stop fertilizing every demon that dare seduce me
maybe I should only deal with illuminated whores

a bleeding elephant ain't got shit on me when my
batteries are recharging
maybe I should just stay this way
I prefer spending more time solo in my cocoon
I inveterately house this inexplicable urge to push people away

maybe I should just strengthen my relationship with mary jane
maybe I should just go bdsm mode on these itchy lolitas
maybe I should just import some customized dolls
maybe I should just treat these juliets the same way I would medusas
maybe I should just get accustomed to unihemispheric sleep
maybe I should just download ultraHD content
maybe I should just put my phone on flight mode and

garden my spirit
maybe I should just go knock on
my favorite ex's door (fully erect cock in hand)
maybe I should just resurrect every addiction I prematurely buried...

Countless Muses

some of them are matrimonially chained
some of them are not
some of them are surprisingly tight down there
some of them have been raped
some of them are recovering addicts
some of them no longer want anything to do with God
some of them used to be inadvisable in their past relationships
some of them are more malleable than prose
some of them showers me with eye candy
some of them has bleeding illness
some of them can't walk in heels
some of them are evil drapped in feminity
some of them are experts at using men
some of them juggles cocks for a living
some of them are corrupt ????? officials
some of them has soul transplants
some of them loves to mark their territories using
unwashed undergarments
some of them are endowed with the rarest of eyes
some of them bath at least three times per day

some of them have unsuccessfully committed suicide
some of them come from financially stable families
some of them
have been aborting since they were in their teens
some of them digs my content
some of them have bastards to feed
some of them naturally smell
some of them have tats and
lots of piercings
some of them can code, kickbox and knit

some of them have done time
some of them used to be groupies
some of them are 7+ years older than me
some of them expertly snore
some of them go both ways
some of them looks like they're in Allah's secret service

some of them are the reason why I
sometimes find myself gestating lines like

1.
my purposefully scarred gladiator
deep in the jaws of her marvelous colosseum;
her entire rome quivering with intense pleasure...

2.
I miss you because your spirit still perfume my dreams
I miss you because my most affluent demons still hum your name
I miss you because (you used to be = halalized heroin) to me.

3.
I fell in love with the fighter in you
I fell in love with the prologue in your eyes
I fell in love with the design
of your lower lip
I fell in love with your brain;
discussing with you is a lot more stimulating than
playing chess with a reverable opponent
I fell in love with your fingers;
everything you touch develops a deeper soul
Oh, I fell in love
with your aura;

You made me realize how much of
a pleasure b-r-e-a-t-h-i-n-g can be
I
fell
in
love
with your unforgettable legs;
they so memorably led me to the one and only Oasis I've ever needed.

4.
between her thighs exist a deconsecrated temple
whoever enters in there absorbs a myriad of unconfessable sins
f**k! I wish her scent wasn't so alluring
not only did I enter uninsulated, I dined. She's
already in my god-damned bloodstream.

5.
today I woke up in time to
witness the birth of this unique day
last night I
supernova'd, discarded the used rubber and
continued with the
exploration of her sacred spaces without parking
she digs that level of "operation"
my fingers
knows her body way better than
the villi of her bath towel shall ever do.
I still haven't washed down her essence from my palate
my tongue (more than
anything else) revels in
embarking on a pilgrimage to her delicious mecca.

6.
I
immeasurably
enjoy witnessing her climax

her holy city
tastes like
undiluted poetry

that mesmerizing disk in God's backyard
was only half grown
when I last made love to my tastiest muse

my fingertips mortally miss her brailled soul
and like believers on the day of pentecost;
my lungs religiously await the fragrance of her inner thighs.

8.
when you tasted yourself from my
one-eyed sower
why did you look up at me with
eyes that flattened every
fortress within me?
you won the hearts of
my most obdurate demons
now your name is the
epitome of royalty in my vessels
_a fatal curse since you're now worlds away in
the confines of your harnesser's ribcage.

9.
I Loved
the way her clothes punctuated her femininity

and I Loved
the way her skin
represented her roots
I
am still in captivity_
captive to the memories of
the things she used to SIMULTANEOUSLY
do to my tip and
shaft.

10.
she was a goddess
I had to spill my magmatic tithe inside her temple
_a deliberate mess.

some of them can perform 100% miracles
some of them owns a variety of sex toys
some of them has spiritual husbands
some of them take meds
some of them can't stand safe sex
some of them are possessed by marine spirits
some of them occasionally sleeps with their bosses...

Afterplay

a familiar cigarette after a crime of passion
a lullabying shower after a night of prostitution
lotus position after creating an inexhaustible work of art

quenching
a soul
on fire...

Just A Few Questions

How would you react if
God commanded you to adopt his shapeshifting son?
How would you react if
you walked in on your mother busy cheating on
your hardworking father?
How would you react if
you realized that you're a product of incest?
How would you react if
you learned that your bride will never be able to
give you a child because of one of the
abortions that she had sometime before your paths crossed?
How would you react if
your hubby impregnated your maid
How would you react if
someone you used to plan your future with
leaked your nudes?
How would you react if
someone you have killed for put a hit on you?

How would you react
if I told you that all your scars
are just one of God's works of art?

How would you react if
you sniffed dick on your wife's breath when she
has never even attempted to go down on you?
How would you react
if your father's killer got a community service sentence?
How would you react
if you learned that the so-called "world map"
is at most a deceitful masterpiece

How would you react if
we informed you that your vote is useless?
How would you react if
your mother got incarcerated for
booing her bitchy domina
How would you react
if your daughter got knocked up by a sodomite?
Hmm???

Creature Of Lust

as the last oasis turns to choking powder
as the devil gains independence
as the sun starts unflinchingly delivering justice
as the intellectual loses appetite for the profound
as the prostitute voluntarily walks into a cloister
as the party venues turn into crime scenes
as the civil servant finds a good reason to
feel offended by your grea$e
as the hired killer starts scrupling
and the philanderer starts lacking pussy
I'd like you to know that
I've always wanted to identify as a human being
I've always wanted to be the archenemy of your sleep
I've always wanted to swap your chip
I've always wanted to be preyed upon by
the Empress Wu of my time

I've always wanted to help Africa have a universal currency
I've always wanted to be deepthroated right in front of
the silk merchant's priceless wife
I've always wanted to take off my
masks (& brass knuckles) and follow Christ
I've always wanted to play a saxophone on a xxx scene
I've always wanted to knock up a pastor's daughter
I've always wanted to be devoured by a shy demoness
I've always wanted to write a letter to my
dearest dead poetess
I've always wanted to write songs for thugs and monks
I've always wanted to play basketball nigh the bermuda triangle
I've always wanted to play house with an immortal woman

I've always wanted to ink an actrice x

Am I sick?

I've always wanted to share my girlfriends (I knew
I was the umpteenth guy between her scented gates
that did not demotivate me,
it instead rendered me more beastly)
I've always wanted to study coral reefs
I've always wanted to be left tf alone 21 hours per day
I've always wanted to paint something inaccrochable with jorja
I've always wanted to taste at least six
XX chromosomed offerings from
every tribe under the sun

I've always wanted
to shoulder your wife's legs and
bury my face in her hair
I've always wanted to perfect my shooting skills in
the capital cities of the world
I've always wanted to elope with a tsarevna
I've always wanted to hunt your instructors
I've always wanted to paint these walls with
somebody's brains
I've always wanted to spend my
days feeding the feminine soul this veined cucumber
I've always wanted to be suffocated by
a churchgoing adulteress' pumpkins

I've always wanted to be immune to
good p%ssy magic (Good p%ssy
can make you commit treason
Good p%ssy can make you abandon your parents

Good p%ssy can make you embezzle
Good p%ssy can make you challenge a frustrated lion
Good p%ssy can make you give prophets the finger
Good p%ssy
can make you play perfect dad to another man's kids
Good p%ssy
can make you do stupid shit on national television

Good p%ssy can make you forget about
the importance of a prenuptial agreement
Good p%ssy can make you bury your armor
Good p%ssy can wean you off your inveterate addictions
Good p%ssy can cuff you in church
or deracinate you out of it
Good p%ssy can plant you in a bloody cult
Good p%ssy can make you unapologetically
break the bro code
Good p%ssy can make you feel like a hall of famer
Good p%ssy can make you marathon
in the rain
on a moonless night

_Good p%ssy, Good p%ssy, GOOD p-u-%-%-y

It can make you lie to your own self
It can make you purchase a goblin
It can make you diss your gods
Good p%ssy
can make you TOLERATE INFIDELITY) I've
always wanted to be a freaking prototype
and
I'd pay whatever to blast each and every
doomsday bunker under the sun.

Dim Nightclubs

dim nightclubs
with polluted air
guarded by bloodthirsty bouncers

dim nightclubs
with fatigued cashiers
who always gives dirty torn change and
unsettling smiles.

affordable whores
with unshaven fields and
unartistically applied makeup (cheap makeup)

affordable whores who can outdrink any fish (on
any given day/night) affordable whores
with a tendency of robbing their clients
affordable whores with no code of honor

dim nightclubs
plagued with affordable whores
keep the poor worker stuck in his unlocked cage

we
for these affordable whores
murder each other in cold blood

and we
in these dim nightclubs
feel more at home than
we have ever felt in any

temple/mosque/gym/marriage...
you name it

Breath Of Life

gotta give music producers Something
to think about
when they're frankensteining
gotta give harnessed womyn Something
to think about
when they're bathing
gotta give the heads of state Something
to think about
when they're doing lines
gotta give the gods
Something to think about
when they're delousing themselves

my ancestors passed me the baton for a reason
every time that the earth shifts I kaizen

listen_

I don't want you to turn lantana
into marijuana for me
I don't want you to makeup the
worm on my hook
I don't want you to protect me from
"partners" who brings nothing to the table (but a
queefing part of their anatomy.)
I don't want you to veneer my nature
I don't want you to lace my prey's drink
I don't want you to capture succubus when she
revisit to hellishly cowgirl me
I don't want you to
do anything to my fiancee's demons

I don't want you to facilitate another
"miscarriage" the next time I fertilize a wrong candidate
I don't want you to "neutralize" those I
deem unworthy of my vote
I don't want you to galvanize my phallus
I don't want you to guide my art to
their erogenous zones
I don't want you to decommission my
conquests

If doing any of that
is going to make you feel like
I OWE YOU.

Balls, Son. Balls

refuse to suck those tits before testing
refuse to vote aimlessly
refuse to jeopardize your legacy
refuse to cum inside her just because
she authorized
refuse to dump it all in God's hands
refuse to abuse drugs for street cred
refuse to wear their colours for endorsements
refuse to sellout for dough

refuse to feign ecstasy
refuse to put your faith in
any of the rubbers you shall find in her lair
refuse to take the pulpit whenever you're feeling filthy
refuse to press the like-button against your own volition
refuse to be vasectomized by the censors
refuse to be stalled by your exes
refuse to be barebacked by the "investors"
refuse to be a predictable bait-taker
refuse to let them in
refuse to pledge your allegiance to their gods

refuse to pinion your spirit
refuse to be the reason why your enemies climax
refuse to let your ancestors down
refuse to parley with savages
refuse to abide by the rules that were crafted to oppress you
refuse to be comfortable in slavery OF ANY KIND

refuse to keep your hands clean whenever it isn't worthy it

refuse to reveal your identity to everyone you meet
refuse to think of God as an unamenable individual
refuse to be kneaded by the zeitgeist
refuse to unsee certain things
refuse to be colonized by your bitch's family
refuse to worry about your opponent's health (you're a prizefighter
not a priest)

refuse to sin against your pigment
refuse to sit in idleness as the dictates of
the world around you mute your heart

refuse to waste her time
show that god-damned cookie no mercy
drill it till it spills all its creamy secrets
drill it till it start queefing with confidence
drill it till it's swollen enough to
appease your sickest gods
drill it till it lyrically ornaments your totem
yes, till it become a possessed poetess (the world
needs more of those)

drill it till it sweats tears of the poppy
drill it till it grants you access to it's bank accounts
drill it till it develop gold medalist mentality
drill it
till it
stammers the
national anthem in reverse
drill it till it forgets all about its ex-lovers
drill it till it lands you in its pantheon
drill it till it stones the neighbors

drill it till it shows an ardent need
for twelve tested exorcists
drill it till it loudly profane
DRILL IT
till it looks at you with a newfound reverence
Oh, DRILL IT.

Long as

long as my multiple rocket launcher still gets hard
long as my pen still has its muses
long as my better half ain't sapping my chi
long as nature is interested in staying my confidant
long as my ancestors are vouching for me
long as salom hasn't been instructed to
request my head on a platter
long as my plenipotentiaries has SOMETHING to lose
long as my contingency plan has a contingency plan
long as my kick game is on point
long as I'm capable of
creating something with an indelible pulse
yes, long as my
semen shall feed not only this generation
long as I know what to do with the
epiphanies that teleports my soul
long as my name unsettles your gods
long as the third gang member still feels welcome within me

long as my heart can still decipher omens
long as I'm still an intuitive animal

long as
your bride still thinks about
this performer whenever she moisturizes her body
long as your daughters are willing to roleplay
long as your worst nightmares
are carrying my fingerprints
long as the law is a sanctimonious bitch that only
open thighs for the affluent
long as solitude still has a

region to cultivate within me

The Fire

a pulsating word in a poem
a jewel lost to the night life
lipstick on snitchy lips
raindrops on a window pane at 07:00 pm
or at 05:10 am
mopane leaves inside a caterpillar
a venerable turd in the house of parliament
a tongue jammed in a bung-hole
jizz in a swallower's mouth
a bucket descending into a well

ah, love

the way my gearbox
responds to the touch of your voice,
whispers your experienced eyes
deploy into my perverted core,
your armour on my floor,
the affirmations I inject
into your system whenever we're physically merged...

"what is love?"

a demon in a married woman's bed
a bullet in an activist's brain
an orgasm that can cause a freelancer in her prime to
sacrifice her sovereignty

judas' lips 'pon Christ's jaw
a blank vote in a ballot box
a fetus in a septic tank
a freedom fighter in a torture chamber
a pad at the convergence of two adorable pillars...

love, love, love

islam
breastfeeding
nuru
death sentences
string theory
baby showers
wavefunctions
make-up sex
squirting medicines
chemical disincorporation
euthanasia
the line "where tf is your testosterone?"
sacred geometry

yes, l-o-v-e

unreported rape cases
pillow talk
fingerprints on any forbidden fruit
the three gang leaders within you and I
the conditions of amnesties

the search for an ikigai
the lies you feed your husband when you're with me
16+ character passwords

postmortem
border control

the hours I spend on inaccrochable art
a journalist sharing a ditch with
an exposé that got him neutralized
toilet paper at work south of your sacrum
a prostitute with a heart full of anhedonia
an uncanceled star about to reappear in your household
a celebrated statesman with a backyard full of
another man's magma for his homeland's sake
a wardrobe turned coffin
one kick that can land your oppressor in the morgue
one song that can throw you into a deep trance
one epiphany that can rapture your soul
one painting that can unshackle your mind
one Bible verse that can breach your pericardium
one friend that can save your marriage
one anthology that can alter your reason for living
one conversation that can boil your blood
one war that can make you permanently blend with God
one prayer that can upgrade your genes
one phone call that can restore the vibrance in your eyes
one grift that can keep you covered for three life times
one church service that can enable you to write a
bestseller on masquerades
one statement that can trap you in front of the cleanest mirror

L-O-V-E

one whisper that can reach your long departed ancestors
one feeling that can sentence you to a life in the studio
one pull that can make you sit with your thoughts for a

full stick of incense when you should be joining your
tossing and turning better half

Love

is e:v:e:r:y:t:h:i:n:g

and NOTHING

I have descried love
in the eyes of a traitor about to fatally leak

and in these very arms I
have held it
in the form of
a sweaty cougar with sapiosexual demons.

"Chipuka"

I was aware
that war
was what you wanted;
its body, not its face.

I was
aware
that sex was what you wanted;
its course, not its consequences.

I was aware
that salvation was what you wanted;
its fruits,
not its roots.

I was aware
that the throne
was what you wanted;
its comfort, not its responsibilities.

I
was aware
that marriage was what you wanted;
its dignity, not its freaking anatomy.

I was aware
that "he" was the one
you wanted;
his surname, not his demons.

I was
aware
that a religion was what you wanted;
its bulwarks, not its ultimatums.

I was aware
that fame was what you wanted;
its aura,
not its appetites.

I was aware that a colony
was what you wanted;
its phat nipples,
not its voice

I was aware
that a friend
was what you wanted;
his shoulder, not his diseases.

I was aware that
intel about the other side
was what you wanted;
its gist, not its provenance.

I was aware
that a scapegoat
was what you wanted;
its blood, not its trust.

you were a very entertaining creature

self-tormented and

unnecessarily conflicted

even my dim-witted pets enjoyed watching you.

Noticed

some go around kissing the sick
some offer scholarships to the underprivileged
some take selfies with outcasts
some make fat offerings in church
some clothe orphans
some wash the senile
some make time to go feed pigeons/ducks
some refuse to take their passenger's' money
some throw a morsel away right before eating
some voluntarily clean houses of worship
some smile at strangers
some bless widows

are you
a good person?

some dig graves for free
some pay million$ for rubbish-art
some takes care of others' spouses
some choose not to knockout their opponents
some fast a lot
some create free xxx websites
some go door to door seeding God's word
some DONATE THEIR OWN BLOOD

do you
want to be a good person?

some provide their "prophets" with intel
some catch bullets for strangers
some benches their elegant clothes
some avoid driving balls to the wall (literally)

Seriously?

(once I recuperate...
once I retire...
once I land on my feet...
once my cock is hard enough...
once I harness the full force of my chi...
once I master the subtle art of mindful living...
once I divorce this insufferable spouse...
once I graduate...
once I start speaking in tongues...
once I wean this child...
once I buy my own weights...
once I hook their hearts...
once I beat this goddamned cancer...
once I secure an unassailable forger...
once I memorize the Qur'an...
once I finish brewing a combustible novel idea...
once I put my hands on that...
once I secure reliable investors...
once I learn how to use...
once I raise enough to approach my in-laws...
once I find it within myself to forgive...
once I see the clouds gathering...

once I turn --...

once I teach my demons placidity...
once I quit gambling...
once I set one foot in...
once my gut feeling give me the greenlight...
once I bring this war to an end...
once my grail is in sight...

once I find a team that truly appreciates my talents...
once I adapt to the darkness...
once I overcome my fear of...)

Ugh, bitch please.

The Thing Is

sometimes I just want someone who can
suck my D-key with zealotry
but sometimes all I want is someone who
can entwine with me at a spiritual level.

sometimes I want someone
who can straddle me and seriously campaign
but sometimes I just want someone who can properly get
on all fours and let me memorably use her.

sometimes I want someone
who can mouth my sacred power source
but sometimes I just want someone who
can drive me jealousy.

sometimes
I want a dirty-mouthed screamer
but sometimes I simply want someone who isn't into
inviting neighbors to our orgasmic duel.

sometimes I want someone who can
leave my intellect with blue balls
but sometimes I just want someone who can make my
inner man tremendously cum.

sometimes I want someone who can let me
watch without touching as she slowly peel herself for
my possessors, but sometimes I just
want someone who cannot even wait for us to get home.

sometimes I want someone who doesn't mind ruining

her manicure on my flesh
but sometimes I
just want the very opposite of a pantheress.

sometimes I want someone I can freely
confide in
but sometimes I only want someone who wanna
cofound the craziest of s3X positions with me and end there.

sometimes I want someone willing to be taken via
more than one passage
but sometimes
I just want someone orthodox.

sometimes I even want someone who must feel pain
in order to gush
but sometimes a fragile lover
do satisfy me.

Don't forget That...

(i)
your tax money is busy commiting genocide.
we're here because of
political hot buttons pressed generations ago.
waking up next to her has no equivalent.
you don't even have to read the folds and
wrinkles of her backdoor to decipher her.
you will find more poon hounds in churches than
in beer halls.
sometimes all you have to do
is shut the f up and concentrate.
your cock is a suicidal pilot.

nobody expects you to be satisfied by
the answers that life thrusts on you.

scars of an artist are often oil wells.
the vaccine is to become your own best form of
entertainment.
if it wakes your brain cells up, it's worthy it.
making God blame you will always be wiser than
making Him blame Himself.
not every university graduate is capable of
defining the word "education"
your legal blunders are your achilles heel, sir!
some creatures can only be activated by
the drums of war.
economic mismanagement is
a higher form of satanism.
most people allow hope to fuck them to death.
I'd rather share her with a butt plug...

(ii)
not everybody who owns a brush and a palette
is a painter
not everybody who strums a guitar
is a musician
not everybody with spikes on their feet
is an track star
not everybody with a story is a novelist
not everybody in a director's chair
has what it takes to become Tyler Perry
not everybody with a Godsent spouse
has a soulmate
not everybody with an ideology
is a leader
not everybody with high IQ
is useful
not everybody flamboyant online
has their shit figured out in life
not everybody who knows herbs is a healer
not everybody with good intentions
is a saint
just as not everybody with blood on their hands
is a criminal

If You Can...

drink till your brain
temporarily loses the ability
to create memories.

tie a joint
and play the ruminant
life can be a shoreless orgasm if you want.

give your convalescent baby mama
another baby just to prove a point,
marriage is a blood sport.

(what if becoming swingers
was the only way through which they
could resuscitate their precious relationship?)

walk away from your prayer mat
change the way you approach this game,
change right fkN now...

harness one of
the whores breastfeeding by the
sacrum of a nightclub.

Must We Always Kill?

of course, we have an empire to defend
of course, we have a ravishing helen to reclaim
of course, we have governments to infiltrate
of course, we have foreign economies to shred
of course, we have a pressing agenda to push
of course, we have infectious ideologies to expunge
of course, we have flammable rumours to neutralize
of course, we have contrabands to smuggle
of course, we have organisations to sabotage
of course, we have minerals to continue looting
of course, we have contracts to seal

of course, we have families to feed
of course, we have a heritage to preserve
of course, we have businesses to engulf
of course, we have precious clients to keep happy
of course, we have records to sell
of course, we have cases to derail
of course, we have dreams to incubate
of course, we have an election to win
of course, we have fatal doubts to dispel
of course, we have a brand to consecrate
of course, we have sacred land to purchase

bloOD!

bloOD!

bloOD!

Avalanches

(stage 1 - crushing and rolling)
BLAME:
the necessity of apostasy
the arousal of desire in old men
the scarcity of honor
the nature of gold
the inventor of hatred
the unexpected absence of the hymen
cosmetic surgery

the woman cowgirling the man at
the helm of your sinking ship

horny schoolgirls in
discombobulatingly altered uniforms
your life coach
nepotism
cock rings
VAR
social media
centrifugal force
D. Rice's right foot
the power of gambling
man-made gods
lethargic spouses
acedia

dependency syndrome on the African continent
any man between a courtesan's thighs while
other men are losing their pith on the battlefield

the killers of cde Muammar Gaddafi
as well as
everyone else who stood back and watched
from a "safe" distance

(stage 2 - halfway down the blunt)
USE/ABUSE:
the first married tunnel I explored
the first live round I fired
the first undefiled boob I inked
the first job I threw away
the first nonhalal haunch I
lost a part of my soul to
the first jersey I knitted
the first kisser who bit me

the first apex predator I
harmoniously
cohabited with

the first addiction I ko'd
the first cougar I peeled
the first spell weaver I saluted
the first toes I mouthed
the first earthmover I operated
the first prostitute I cuddled with
the first manuscript I incinerated
the first angelic creature I irrumated
the first hoop I gloriously assaulted
the first wall I adorned
the first workmate I nearly knocked up
the first democracy I condemned
the first slough I premeditatedly revisited

the first unhangable work of art I vaulted
the first sapphist I bathed with
the first will I wrote

(stage 3 - after nearly burning my fingertips)
RELAX:
you don't need championship rings
you don't need the love of a cultured virgin
you don't need to shake that guy's regal hand
you don't need to devour any of those TED talks
you don't need a raging nostalgia for anything
you don't need to become a vegetarian
you don't need to unblock that pastor
you don't need to join those subscribers
you don't need bodyguards from any special forces
you don't need to fill up
another stadium/womb/condom...

you don't need that armband
you don't need to conjure spirits from
neither the past nor the future
you don't need a rebound love
you don't need to lose your sleep over whatever the
shitstem expects of you
you don't need to study abroad
you don't need to consult any seer
you don't need the warmth of a tailored apology
you don't need to jam your day in the
rectum of negativity
you don't need to question the nature of your reality
on a daily basis

you don't need new trade routes

you don't need the ambience of
a familiar confession booth

you don't need the wetness
of an anointed seedbed

you don't need videos of them scissoring
you don't need some chewing tobacco with which to
rouse your earthed ancestors
you don't need a pet
with a soul three times the size of New York city
you don't need new meditation techniques
you don't need the services of
a toe-curlingly amazing masseuse

what you need
is total presence

slow the f%ck down

b
r
r
r
e
a
t
h
e

Bloody Cross Section

I've been suicidal;
I've skinny dipped in flowers of the night.

I've been an actor;
I've absent-mindedly taken oaths.

I've been an idolater;
my tongue has pedestaled clits.

I've been a false god;
I've facialized your daughters and sisters.

I've been a dog;
I've revisited some exes.

I've been a deserter.
I've been spooked by the prospect of commitment.

I've been a deceiver;
I've always felt safer behind a mask.

I've been a vampire;
I timely realized that it all belongs to animals of prey

I've been a homebreaker;
I've always thrived on the forbidden fruit.

I've been a trojan horse;
I've been dramatically used.

I've been pathetic;
I've worked towards the impossible.

I've been a self-sabotager;
I've sunk my haustorium all the way into God's tenth.

Somewhere Between Doomed And Privileged

exposed to sanctified chaos
exposed to brutalist elegance
exposed to inseminators of ideologies
exposed to negotiable whores that looks
worse than painted corpses
exposed to mouths deadlier than weapons of war

what now?
must I go assume the vajrasana pose on a mountain top?
must I put a ring on a boobed time bomb?
must I call a forbidden fruit over to my place (and
temporarily determine her style of
walking?)

exposed to viruses by profitmongering racists
exposed to feral water spirits
exposed to flabbergastingly insecure lovers
exposed to metamorphosed pharisees
exposed to bad breath
exposed to heavily edited truths
exposed to insatiable data miners
exposed to sadistic enforcers
exposed to frivolous leaders
exposed to parasitic relatives
exposed to distractive church mates

exposed to catastrophically misplaced hearts
exposed to soulless capitalists
exposed to very attractive propositions
exposed to dirty money
exposed to targeted individuals

exposed to eyes thirstier than the blade of the guillotine
exposed to incurable systems and
xenomorphic creatures

exposed

to transfenestrated angels, perfidious renegades,
gullible adjudicators, well done trannies,
irredeemable gamblers,
residual presences,
vindictive children, sick blessers,
pastors with fragile egos,
unwanted fighters, chameleonic friends,
diplomatic demons,
indefatigable spouses, hellish passengers
suicidal guardians, drug dealing lawmen,
deprived perverts

exposed
to extremely beautiful women with black hole lives.

in an ocean of hypotheticals;
a man is more than just a god in
a custom-made hell.

Vixen

you do not love me
you never loved me
you love comfort
you love sweet fiction
you love the perquisites of
riding superstar d!ck

you love the spotlight
you love silk sheets and
five star-breakfast in bed
you love receiving thorough rim-jobs
yeah, you love being lustfully licked (bean to
back door.)

you love tipping like the queen of the gods
you love making love under the influence
you love supercars, designerwear, rare wines,
after-parties and
purses that comes with
ridiculous price tags

precious stones are something you literally worship

there is no limit to the things you can do just to net #likes

you love feeling like a shrine
you love giving 'em something to jerk off to
you love having em wrapped around your little finger

well, guess what?

Memory

1. the katana along her spine
2. the dreamcatcher on her left shoulder
3. the majestic st. paul's cathedral with an
apex flanked by her mesmerizingly aureoled twins
4. the paradise-ahead sign below her navel
5. & 6. the moon spooning the star symbol
below the eye of providence
on her nape
7. the "hope is a thing with feathers..." verse
on her left inner arm
8. swallows in flight on the roof of
her right foot
9. the "try abusing your goddess" order
in japanese characters
on the region between her venus dimples and
her butt cheeks
10. (she
currently has ten tattoos.) the tenth one
is visible only when...

Appetizing AF

you could almost
see the flow
of energy
in her body
using the necked eye

she
moved with
marvelous sprightfulness and
utmost gracefulness
_a triggered ballerina portraying
heaven's breath.

Unhooked

He no longer blazes
He no longer answers unknown callers
He no longer shoves himself into random cockpits
He no longer religiously follows any sports league
He no longer persecutes any of the
plants that grows in his front yard
He no longer watches corruptive content
He no longer possesses the patience for
door to door soul-fishing
He no longer pursues romance
He no longer needs a date to plumb a woman's
crude depths
He no longer debates the Bible with anyone
He no longer touches his cellphone upon waking up
He no longer belongs to any pack
He no longer submits his entrails to strangers online
He no longer feeds the ballot boxes
He no longer trims his soul for rousing reviews

some feel he's lost his head

some have simply dismissed him as
an ungrateful bastard

and some
are those who have found everything they needed to
publicly crucify him

He
no longer
gives a fvck.

02:57 a.m. Already

can it be my habit of
never leaving the house without a
round in the chamber?
can it be the voltage of
the lips that gleaned my...
can it be the quality
of the kicks I walk in?
can it be the calibre
of my bars?
can it be the color
of my eyes?
can it be the humidity of my better half's pussy?

can it be the grade
of the leaves I used to serve my brain cells?
can it be the minds I love elucubrating with?
can it be the entertainers I prefer?
can it be the concoctions in my system?
can it be my choice of words and
timing?
can it be the wars that have licked my blood?
can it be my scars and
body art?
can it be my
ability to use literary devices as drug paraphernalia?
can it be the masks I owe my life to?
can it be the age of my pha...raoh's favorites?

can it be my ability to
lure hearts out of their shells for the

evilest of reasons?
can it be the consciousness of my fangs?
can it be the mother tongue of
my knuckles?
can it be the house manager of my heart?
can it be my attempt to turn stone into wet silk?
can it be the portal I shall be disvirgining tonight?
can it be the pariahs I pray with?
can it be the night clubs I prowl in?
can it be the fugitives I harbour in my inner sanctum?

can it be this award-winning photo of
a vulture waiting
for a starving little girl to die before
feasting on her godforsaken corpse?
can it be my relationship with the
gods of my enemies?

can it be the covenants that my ancestors got us into
way before my arrival?

can it be the rosary on my chest?
can it be the skeletons in my closet?
can it be the ex attempting to hex my manhood?
can it be the voices of my savings accounts?
can it be the condom that recently betrayed me?
can it be the innocence I've brazenly sent to the guillotine?
can it be my ability to breathe life into symbols
and
mobilise God's troops

I have a tendency
of using the triumvirate in my briefs as

my puppet government
Can it be that?

Status quo

the dogs
are eating used sanitary towels
and diapers.
the girls
are lowering paying strangers' zippers
the package
isn't gonna gobble its own self.
the shark
might astronomically fuckup, but
rest assured, it won't give the crown up.
the average politician runs around with an
erect cock in hand
and eventually die with blue balls
the brilliant one gets away with rape.
woke donkeys cuckold stallions on a daily basis
Oh, people choose
to act as if they
do not know what fattened the pig.

Preprogrammed

wine collection
art collection
wife collection
sneaker collection
sex toy collection
car collection
music collection
drug collection
pxrn collection
gun collection
lingerie collection
timepiece collection
golf club collection
fishing hook collection
mitten collection
passport collection
spacesuit collection
sword collection
satchel collection
sock collection
skull collection

because we have monsters to feed
because we have abysses to appease
because we have mind damaging voices to shush
because we're sick

because we're cursed
because we're powerless
because we're possessed
because the truth penetrates better when circumcised

guess who has the best grass in this area?

For Hours

some nights I feel like
painting something 100% inaccrochable
some nights I feel like cuddling with the Holy Bible

some nights I feel like skinny dipping in a pregnant river
some nights I feel like making love to sativa

some nights
I feel like shapeshifting

some nights I feel like dialing an ex
some nights I feel like visiting booby-trapped websites

some nights I feel like
mercilessly inking my own body
some nights I feel like
drowning myself in my study

some nights I feel like renaming the stars
some nights I feel like discoursing with my scars

was l born like this?
by whose code am I programmed?

some nights I feel like asking dangerous questions
some nights I feel like crossing the goddamned rubicon

some nights I feel like surrendering myself to my
darkest urges
some nights I feel like renovating my cage

sometimes a simple act of kindness
is way more satisfying than
the most earthshaking orgasm

some nights I feel like handwriting letters
to my unborn children

some nights I feel like
doing something more Christian than
going to church every Sunday

some nights
I feel like quenching my hardware with
live performances by some
extremely addictive
predators

and some nights I
feel like bareknucklingly torturing punching bags

If You Cannot Do It For Yourself

then do it for the flag that flies above your head
or for the woman who always submissively
opens her legs
to embrace your tyranny
or for the seed YOU spewed
or for the bones of your ancestors
or for a stillborn that would have been
immeasurably grateful to have what you have
or for the elixir trapped in the heart of a
subterranean stone

or for the girl selling her body for a
one dollar plate of sadza & offals

or for the innocent prisoner who just got
raped all night
or for a whistle-blower who just dropped dead of
a mysterious heart attack.

Decryption

I'm not an evolved ape; I'm my mother's son
I'm not my mother's son; I'm Zimbabwean
I'm not Zimbabwean; I'm African
I'm not African; I'm a human being
I'm not a human being; I'm an earthly king
I'm not an earthly king; I'm
a key-grain of the universe
I'm not a key-grain of the universe;
I'm an ever metamorphing question

picked up by drugs
trained by ex divine forces
advised by omens

conceived in the liver of a war
forged in the jaws of oblivion
and tested in the realms of the illuminated

Becoming "Him"

what if you
spend the rest of your days
collecting unfinished paintings,
producing music that targets the
undying part of men,
capturing whatever touches you differently,
fucking the most extraordinary females of the species,
racing rare cars,
having barefooted contact with sacred land,
bathing in waterfalls and natural pools,
conceiving architectural miracles,
practicing deep-sea fishing,
hunting big game,
mastering ancient and
endangered languages,

unsparingly studying (the human brain,
boxers, heisters, cats, religions, economies,
temptresses, viruses, cartels, stock markets,
security organizations, cultural bulldozers, fractals,
landforms, ecosystems, civilisations, wars, medicine,
governments, ideological movements such as jihadism...)

forging swords,
correcting history,
decrypting the pluriverse,

crossbreeding (livestock,
peasants, athletes, world leaders...)

seeking inspiration in casinos,

whorehouses and
jungles?

Wait

do not kill me for refusing
to dance on my enemy's grave
do not kill me for
not ****** till I
had a turf to protect
do not end me for being interested in the
supersecrets of the vatican
do not kill me for harvesting your daughter's field
without your blessing
do not kill me
for processing some banned content during a church service
do not kill me simply because
your precious wife
just reminded me
that NOTHING
is out of
my reach.

do not kill me because my chats with her
make up priceless works of adult literature

do not kill this speaker in order to
mute the demonic ones in your head
do not take my life to cover your gambling debts

do not lynch me for "heresy" when
you'd rather endorse me
do not kill me to clinch a promotion
do not kill me to prove your worth to your asylum providers.

do not kill me in order to inherit my shit
do not kill me for a reward
I'm not the type whose blood can be spilled for gain

what have "they" promised you?
what are you looking for?

why kill me when
exile is a far much brutal sentence
do not kill me for not showing up at your
parties, rallies, funerals, and so forth

do not kill me in order to sabotage my projects
do not kill me in order to quarantine my worldview
do not kill me for attempting to eclipse
modigliani's nu couche
using that busty bride of yours
you mustn't kill me for emancipating your bitch.

kill me for something else if you will
kill me for interceding for the souls of your brainwashers
horizontalize me for publicly unmasking that
so-called democracy of yours
haul me to the firing wall for
satirizing the status quo, but
don't even think of it for my
dismissing you as a spineless sycophant
or for your failure to tame the mother of your children.

do not make me disappear for addressing
the turd between your ears instead of
the one plastered on the sole of your shoe.

Oh! you scooped a venereal disease from
one of my conquests?
I have nothing to do with that.

do not get rid of me for the absence of
either jealous or compersion in my eyes
do not kill me for bombing your palace of ignorance
do not cut the string of life on me for my forefathers' fuck ups
do not kill me for savagely sinking my canines in
the hand sweeping moldy crumbs my way
do not kill me for climbing out of an inferno healthier than ever
do not kill me for converting your heir

do not kill me for not thanking you for your service (we
believe that you...)
do not kill me for questioning the
authenticity of your life's work
do not kill me for having faith in both_
Christ's blood and these herbs
do not kill me for asserting
that adult entertainment really has
done more good than harm to the species
do not kill me for letting my Bible cohabit with
a copy of...

do not kill me simply because I have stronger melanin than you

but

if any of you is to neutralize me
do it manly
do not administer poisoned medication to me
or contract a witch to do your dirty work

babe, don't murder me for being immune to your
love portions
comrade, don't spill my blood for
choosing to preserve what's left of my innocence
mama, don't denounce your son for marrying a veteran
my fellow earthlings, please do not crucify me for
saying "no!" to being governed by terrestrial perspectives, but
he or she
who is convinced that humanity
has a better shot at survival without my kind
please feel free to start with me on your
philanthropic crusade

(my dear clansmen,
consider euthanizing me should Job's fate
befall me.)

Dilemma

I hate the fact that you're
the refuge I find myself immersed within when
my beloved and I aren't vibing
I hate the fact that verbal intercourse with you
is like both a stroll in the park and
fresh water down my throat amid an
unforgiving desert - easy and lifesaving.

I hate the fact that being entwined with you
beats any magical drug known to mankind

I hate the fact
that you know me better than her
you sync with me way better
than her
and I hate the fact that
when I'm pillowed on your lap
my vulnerability is neither abused nor
misinterpreted
O, I hate the fact that your smile
is like Jesus' word to the
deadly tempest in me
I really hate it
I hate the fact that your eyes
(oases for my subconscious
dojos for my intellect)
affords me the pleasure of
experiencing novalunosis quite intensely_
I hate the fact that
the pulp of my inner man

finally carries someone's fingerprints and
they aren't the fingerprints of
my mother's daughter in law.

last week your name
nearly escaped my lips
as I was about to cream her pie

I hate the fact that I'd rather reserve my
life force for you
O, it's not just the vibrations and
anointing which you bring to my bed
it's the voltage with which you
use your eyes on me
it's the grace with which you come into
contact with my rough edges
it's the depth of your response whenever I
greet your gluteal cleft using my phallus...

December 03

there are those who
never do well in the cutthroat race
not me, I mercilessly won.
there are those who
don't make it through those very tricky nine
months in the womb
I graduated gestation
(shit! I really survived.)
there are those
who upon the midwife's bed
arrive without what it takes to carry on
I wasn't one of them.
there are those who never swim in
a mermaid's territory and
safely make it back home
I countlessly did.
there are those who never survive a venomous snakebite
I'm one of the fiercely lucky ones
(03 december 2011) I survived

I survived to be here today
dealing with all this shit I'm facing
with a smile that looks like something else.

NPCs

no free will
no fire in the belly
no guts
their balls has been chewed by the system
and they have long pledged their unborn
to the ultimate regime
now they walk around flaunting receipts of
their trade with mf mephistopheles
zero shame
zero consciousness
zero suspicion
they are a barebacked breed
and they're everywhere_
in banks
in parks
in houses of parliament
in academic institutions
on their masters' farms
underground in their enslavers' tunnels
in houses of religion (more
than anywhere else)

Concisely

they have guns
we have the gold

they have factories
we have the diamonds

they have currency
we have the oil

they have softwares
we have the platinum

they have stadiums
we have the players

they have viruses
we have guinea pigs (mirror mirror...)

they have beds
we have the women

the problem, the tragedy, our TRAGEDY
is that they have the balls

and we
the freaking bellies.

Yes.

Got Game?

you don't ask someone, "what makes you laugh or smile?"
you observantly spend time with them.

you don't petition mother earth to
surrender her jewels to you;
you respectfully rob her.

you don't command the gods to
grace you with the rains;
you seduce them.

you don't...
for life and all it's avenues
strictly requires the subtle arts.

otherwise, your wife
will belong to the public
and your throne will soon serve as a urinary.

Consider Yourself Warned

ask me for money
ask me to sacrifice a comrade
ask me for undeserved forgiveness
ask me for a night with my grail
ask me for a day in my flashiest kicks
ask me to vote like an amnesiac
ask me for my plate as I'm
washing my hands to dig in
ask me to pay your bullies a visit pro bono
ask me to take an oath at gunpoint
ask me to cheat on my soulmate
ask me to tongue that forested cat

dare even ask me to
abstain from gambling

just don't ever ask me to
wake up at **any** ungodly hour of
the morning
(why interrupt my communion with the divine)
that shit assaults my brain and
deranges the dragon within.

don't be so suicidal
I cannot hang up on the gods for Anything
(not even for aromatic dew-laced pussy lips.)

Remember

you have gills; you're a child of the ocean
you have a limitless heart; you're a poet
you have corrupted that renewable soul;
you have a specific reason for living
the sky is your playground; have you forgot
that the phoenix
is your brother?
suicide is for the blasphemers; sit quietly
in an improvised temple and
mindfully hatch
God intends to visit your lungs;
anticipate Him,
be found unclogged

It's Time

the song is looking for someone to touch
the wild flower is looking for a spirit to upgrade
the wind is politely inviting you, "who
is in the mood for a dance?"

the rain
is searching for the burdened to set free.
Christ's ghost is interested in a friendship
with someone willing to defiantly smile
can you honor a symbiosis?

there is
very little integrity being
practiced in the world today

there are way nobler religions than violence and indecency
a haiku has arms big enough to rebalance a collapsing mountain
the sea can perfectly fit on a prayer rug

my sketchpad is unmistakably horny tonight
I'm always less lonely in the presence of
titillating ideas, but
there are very few things I won't sacrifice for
the best fellowship in bed.

The Ark

I give perpetual Orgasms
and Soulgasms
to those who aren't selfish
I salute
those who deserve my acknowledgement
I venerate
those who have earned my respect
I give money
to those I trust with the fruits of my labor

I restitute
those who might contribute to my perdition
I go to war
for those who honor my core
I never dismiss the rubber unless
my heart is already compromised
I unhesitatingly fashion with
the robes off my own back
those who require bait to
get hooked on God

I share my side pieces
with my soulmate
I give warning shots after the kill shot
to whoever threatens my sovereignty
I habitually subscribe
to whatever nourishes my qi
I ensnare whatever I must ensnare
for the welfare of my offspring
I forsake my ego

in the name of nationalism
I rouse God's nostrils for
divine favours
I carouse with members of the defenestrated family
in order to extract heaven's top-secrets
I print my disturbing works on my clothing
for reasons I do not feel like sharing today

I refill nocturnal business women's cups for free
simply because I'm a feminist
I juggle jobs like a gluttonous mofo, but
take care of strangers like I'm Christ's successor
I do not like voicing in the house of the Lord;
I'm aware of some of His allergies
I struggle not at perceiving the invisible;
I shoulder an inventor's brain
I watch what enters my chest way more than
that which peristaltically finds its way into
my stomach
because I
carry the ark of God within this rib cage
I'm continuously bemused
for the universe I live in has multiple g-spots

the prospect of apostasy
seduces my mind whenever unexpurgated evil makes a
cuckold of me
because...

Things That Mobilize My Pen

some of them prioritize jewelry over acres of land
some of them demand libation before opening
their ears to a petition
some of them improve in elasticity when excited
some of them bleed turquoise
some of them are cursed with nocturnality
some of them are indefinitely doing time in
their own skulls
some of them are as good as infibulated
some of them love the way I
memorize their features while they are asleep

some of them plan to turn me into a hybrid vampire
some of them are addicted to weaponized love
some of them can attain a
mind-blowing high without touching a drug
some of them can wholesale bullshit to a politician
some of them can bag 100K likes within an hour
some of them are forced to swallow poison on a daily basis
some of them were built on millions of
wooden logs driven deep into the seafloor
some of them have nuclear weapons and
sleeper agents in
every strategic corner of the globe
some of them intend to build forest cities
some of them won't mind if
humanity nears extinction tomorrow
some of them cannot sleep without
exchanging bodily fluids with hell's future fuel

some of them have a lot in common with spiderwebs
some of them can do 0-400-0 km/h in 42seconds
some of them are going to stop visiting me
after reading this

some of them
make me enjoy relapsing (you
learn a lot
about a woman
from what she does with
your magma
once it's in her mouth.)

some of them are endowed with
diehard cone-shaped boobs
some of them carry the scent of heresy
some of them aren't spiritually circumcised
some of them have a tendency of repenting during penetration
some of them lost their rear tightness by accident
some of them have heads of state and bishops at
the tips of the strings attached to their nimble fingers
(some of them influence government policies from
behind the scenes)
some of them are blessed with
pumpkins mesmerizing enough to temporarily paralyze a man's
sorrows

some of them genuinely give a
fvck about the fate of my spirit and
the physique of my wallet

some of them act like they used to court gods
in their past lives

some of them are terrifyingly obsessed with
where I put my cock whenever my cell is unreachable
some of them got into my life through
a friend of a friend
some of them has been involved in
game-changing gangbangs
some of them are very successful tax evaders
some of them survived abortion attempts
some of them has quite a way of
weighing my magazine

(which drug do you prefer using?
which race do you prefer rawing?
which gender do you prefer hiring?
which religion do you prefer practicing?
which political party do you prefer tolerating?)

some of them can spot fish from great distances
some of them are just timeless miracles of
architectural geometry
some of them are considered hackproof
some of them ass lick the angel of death for a living
some of them can tame the spherical leather like
some legendary brazilians
some of them can
ejaculate over 1100 killers per minute
some of them know the horror of
being voted out of something they founded and
countlessly bled for

some of them are in the business of
syphoning the future from juvenile clan-banks
some of them can strike faster than a cobra and

outdance their own shadow
some of them travel the world raping all kinds of huntresses
some of them are just lucky liers (the rubber
do sometimes infuse me with
the courage of a drunken army
O, what have I become?)

some of them
can thrive just fine without importing anything
some of them only crave things other
people have failed to love
some of them need a little blood in the water to
swim past writer's block
some of them fishes with war generals and
seasoned professors
some of them are eager to merge their bloodline
with mine
(last night
she kissed me with a mouth full of
half-chewed food)

some of them reengineered my psyche (each
nipple was as sacred as the kaaba
my hajj-worthy tongue
commenced tawaf around
the one closest to her heartbeat
I might have looked like
a tiger muzzledeep into
its secured prey, but
the truth is she was my mecca and
loving her like that was the honor of
my life.)

Mmap New African Poets Series

If you have enjoyed *Juices Of The Forbidden Fruit,* consider these other fine books in the **Mmap New African Poets Series** from *Mwanaka Media and Publishing:*

I Threw a Star in a Wine Glass by Fethi Sassi
Best New African Poets 2017 Anthology by Tendai R Mwanaka and Daniel Da Purificacao
Logbook Written by a Drifter by Tendai Rinos Mwanaka
Mad Bob Republic: Bloodlines, Bile and a Crying Child by Tendai Rinos Mwanaka
Zimbolicious Poetry Vol 1 by Tendai R Mwanaka and Edward Dzonze
Zimbolicious Poetry Vol 2 by Tendai R Mwanaka and Edward Dzonze
Zimbolicious: An Anthology of Zimbabwean Literature and Arts, Vol 3 by Tendai Mwanaka
Under The Steel Yoke by Jabulani Mzinyathi
Fly in a Beehive by Thato Tshukudu
Bounding for Light by Richard Mbuthia
Sentiments by Jackson Matimba
Best New African Poets 2018 Anthology by Tendai R Mwanaka and Nsah Mala
Words That Matter by Gerry Sikazwe
The Ungendered by Delia Watterson
Ghetto Symphony by Mandla Mavolwane
Sky for a Foreign Bird by Fethi Sassi
A Portrait of Defiance by Tendai Rinos Mwanaka
Zimbolicious: An Anthology of Zimbabwean Literature and Arts, Vol 4 by Tendai Mwanaka and Jabulani Mzinyathi
When Escape Becomes the only Lover by Tendai R Mwanaka
ويَسـهَرُ اللَّيلُ عَلَى شَـفَتي...وَالغَمَام by Fethi Sassi

A Letter to the President by Mbizo Chirasha
This is not a poem by Richard Inya
Pressed flowers by John Eppel
Righteous Indignation by Jabulani Mzinyathi:
Blooming Cactus by Mikateko Mbambo
Rhythm of Life by Olivia Ngozi Osouha
Travellers Gather Dust and Lust by Gabriel Awuah Mainoo
Chitungwiza Mushamukuru: An Anthology from Zimbabwe's Biggest Ghetto Town by Tendai Rinos Mwanaka
Zimbolicious: An Anthology of Zimbabwean Literature and Arts, Vol 5 by Tendai Mwanaka
Because Sadness is Beautiful? by Tanaka Chidora
Of Fresh Bloom and Smoke by Abigail George
Shades of Black by Edward Dzonze
Best New African Poets 2020 Anthology by Tendai Rinos Mwanaka, Lorna Telma Zita and Balddine Moussa
This Body is an Empty Vessel by Beaton Galafa
Between Places by Tendai Rinos Mwanaka
Best New African Poets 2021 Anthology by Tendai Rinos Mwanaka, Lorna Telma Zita and Balddine Moussa
Zimbolicious: An Anthology of Zimbabwean Literature and Arts, Vol 6 by Tendai Mwanaka and Chenjerai Mhondera
A Matter of Inclusion by Chad Norman
Keeping the Sun Secret by Mariel Awendit
سِجلٌّ مَكتُوبٌ لتَائه by Tendai Rinos Mwanaka
Ghetto Blues by Tendai Rinos Mwanaka
Zimbolicious: An Anthology of Zimbabwean Literature and Arts, Vol 7 by Tendai Rinos Mwanaka and Tanaka Chidora
Best New African Poets 2022 Anthology by Tendai Rinos Mwanaka and Helder Simbad
Dark Lines of History by Sithembele Isaac Xhegwana
a sky is falling by Nica Cornell

Death of a Statue by Samuel Chuma
Along the way by Jabulani Mzinyathi
Strides of Hope by Tawanda Chigavazira
Young Galaxies by Abigail George
Coming of Age by Gift Sakirai
Mother's Kitchen and Other Places by Antreka. M. Tladi
Best New African Poets 2023 Anthology by Tendai Rinos Mwanaka, Helder Simbad and Gerald Mpesse
Zimbolicious Anthology Vol 8 by Tendai Rinos Mwanaka and Mathew T Chikono
Broken Maps by Riak Marial Riak
Formless by Raïs Neza Boneza
Of poets, gods, ghosts. Irritants and storytellers by Tendai Rinos Mwanaka
Ethiopian Aliens by Clersidia Nzorozwa
In The Inferno by Jabulani Mzinyathi
Who Told You To Be God by Mariel Awendit
Nobody Loves Me by Abigail
The Stories of Stories by Nkwazi Mhango
Nhorido by Siphosami Ndlovu and Tinashe Chikumbo
Best New African Poets 10th Anniversary: Selected English African Poets by Tendai Rinos Mwanaka
Best New African Poets 10th Anniversary: Interviews and Reviews of African Poets by Tendai Rinos Mwanaka
Best New African Poets 10th Anniversary: African Languages and Collaborations by   Tendai Rinos Mwanaka
ANTOLOGIA DOS MELHORES "NOVOS" POETAS AFRICANOS 10º Aniversário: Poetas Africanos Da Língua Portuguesa Selecionados by Lorna Telma Zita and Tendai Rinos Mwanaka
ABRACADABRA, by Olivia Ngozi Osuoha
DES MEILLEURS "NOUVEAUX" POÈTES AFRICAINS 10ᵉ Anniversaire : Poètes africains d'expression française by Geraldin Mpesse and Tendai Rinos Mwanaka
Taurai Amai by Cosmas Tasvika Manhanhanha

Nhemeramutupo by Oscar Gwiriri
Ntombentle: Selected Poems by Sithembele Isaac Xhegwana

www.ingramcontent.com/pod-product-compliance
Lightning Source LLC
Chambersburg PA
CBHW071007160426
43193CB00012B/1957